Snippets of Paul Gascoigne

Dave Farnham

DISCLAIMER

While every effort has been made to ensure the
information in this book is correct, human error is always a
possibility and therefore the author cannot accept
responsibility for any inaccuracies.

CONTENTS

INTRODUCTION

In the world of sport there are a few personalities who become household names, recognised even by those people not interested in the subject. Can there be anyone unaware of such names as Andy Murray, Lewis Hamilton, Tiger Woods, Mohammed Ali or David Beckham, even if they don't know much about their chosen fields?

To this list can be added Paul Gascoigne who, like an earlier footballer, George Best, is as well known for what has happened to him off the field as on it.

Much has been said about him; much also has been said *by* him. In this book I've gathered many memorable quotes in an attempt to shed light on a man who has been in and out of the headlines at both ends of the newspapers, for a quarter of a century.

BIO

Paul John Gascoigne

Nickname: Gazza

1967 Born Gateshead, May 27th. Father, John, was a hod-carrier; mother, Carol, factory worker. Named after Paul McCartney and John Lennon.

1978 Attended Heathfield Senior High School, Gateshead.

1980 Signed by Newcastle United as a schoolboy player.

1983 Signed as an apprentice player by Newcastle United.

1984 -85 Captain of Newcastle United's youth team, helping them to win FA Youth Cup, scoring twice in Final away at Watford.

1985 April 13th Played for the first team as a substitute against Queens Park Rangers. Signed up by Jack Charlton on a two-year contract at £120 a week.

1985 Willie McFaul took over as manager of Newcastle United and played Gascoigne in opening game. He continued to play in first eleven, scoring his first home goal on September 21st, against Oxford United.

1985 -86 Gascoigne scored a total of nine goals during the season, which saw Newcastle United finish in 11th place in First Division (now Premier League). He was featured on the front cover of Rothmans Football Year Book.

1987 Joined England Under-21 team and played 13 times for them, scoring against Morocco in his first game.

1988 Named Professional Footballers' Association (PFA) Young Player of the Year. Received offers from Manchester United and Tottenham Hotspur. Promised Alex Ferguson he would sign for Manchester but eventually signed for Spurs for British record fee of £2,200,000. According to Ferguson, Spurs clinched the deal by buying a house for Gascoigne's family.

1989 Gained place in full England squad.

1988 – 89 Scored seven goals for Spurs under Terry Venables, in season which ended with Spurs in 6th place.

1989 – 90 Spurs finished 3rd in First Division and Gascoigne was named their player of the year as well as becoming BBC Sports Personality of the Year.

1990 Played for England in World Cup. Received second yellow card during game with Germany and was seen in tears by TV viewers.

1990 – 91 Named on PFA Team of the Year. Tottenham reached FA Cup Final against Nottingham Forest, Gascoigne having scored six goals in the competition.

Fifteen minutes into the final he committed a serious foul in the penalty area, severely damaging his own right knee in the process. He left the field in great pain, Spurs going on to finish as winners in extra time.

1991 – 92 Gascoigne missed the whole season because of his knee injury. He had been about to sign a contract with Italian club Lazio at the time of the injury and there was much newspaper speculation about his future.

1992 Signed with Lazio for fee of £5,500,000. His contract gave him £22,000 per week.

1992 – 93 Made debut for Lazio September 27th against Genoa. Match broadcast live on TV in UK as well as Italy. He had variable success on the field but Lazio finished fifth in the League, gaining them a place in European competition, their first in sixteen years.

1993 Ordered by manager Dino Zoff to lose weight before the season started – he was considered two stone overweight. He managed it with extreme dieting.

1994 April, broke leg during a match.

1995 Decided to leave Italy and signed for Glasgow Rangers.

1995 – 96 Gascoigne and Rangers had a very successful season, Gascoigne scoring nineteen goals, being named PFA Scotland's player of the year. Rangers won both the Scottish League and the Scottish Cup.

1996 July, Married girlfriend Sheryl Failes.

1996 – 97 Another successful season for Gascoigne and Rangers, winning League and League Cup. However, he began to use alcohol excessively.

1997 He got a five match ban following violent conduct in a game against Celtic.

1997 – 98 Rangers won no trophies, Gascoigne scoring only three goals in the whole season. He caused trouble with Celtic fans, mocking them from the pitch and was fined £20,000 by Rangers. He also received death threats as a result of his actions. (There has long been tension between 'Protestant' Rangers and 'Catholic' Celtic).

1998 March, signed by manager Bryan Robson for Middlesbrough, who were promoted to the Premier Division at the end of the season. Gascoigne started suffering blackouts and spent time in rehab.

1998 Played last-ever game for England against Italy in World Cup group stage. Adverse publicity about Gascoigne in tabloid newspapers resulted in the manager, Glen Hoddle, deciding to drop him for the rest of the tournament.

1998 Divorced by Sheryl because of domestic violence, admitted by Paul.

1998 – 99 A good season for both Gascoigne and Middlesbrough, finishing sixth in Premier Division.

1999 – 2000 Broke his elbow during a ferocious tackle on Aston Villa player Boateng, being fined £5.000 by the FA and banned for three games. At end of season, was given a free transfer to Everton.

2000 – 01 Suffered bouts of depression as well as injuries. Treated at alcohol rehab unit in Arizona.
2001 – 02 Resumed his place in Everton squad and scored

his last goal as a top-flight footballer on November 3rd against Bolton Wanderers. Injured soon after and out of action for three months. Eventually transferred to Burnley but left after two months.

2003 Signed for Chinese team Gansu Tianma as player and coach and scored in his first game. But depression and alcohol again meant time in rehab (again in USA) and he left that job.

2004 Signed by Boston United, in English League Two, as player and coach, but left after three months.

2004 Co-wrote book *Gazza: My Story*.

2005 Signed as manager by non-league Kettering Town but sacked after thirty-nine days.

2004 – 14 Continued to fight alcoholism and mental illness.

ABOUT HIMSELF

"I've got a bit of money in the bank. I'm quite comfortable."

*

"If the fans want me out, I'll put my hands up and leave. Like a proper man. I won't make excuses, I'll leave."

*

"I never refused an autograph, never refused to buy someone a drink. Now I'm learning to say I've got other things on, instead of doing it and wondering why."

*

"I'm going to do things when they are right for me."

*

"If I want to be a better person for whoever is in my life, I have to learn."

*

"I don't really do pranks any more. I have a laugh in the dressing room here, where it's safe, and the guys don't go to the papers and tell them what I've done."

*

"I never predict anything, and I never will."

*

"I take responsibility for myself and what I do now."

*

"Hopefully everybody will just let me get on with my life. I'm going to."

*

"I just wanted the day to pass and the next day to come and then I wanted that one to pass. It was a horrible cycle. I felt so close to having to pack the game in."

*

When his career in football came to an end:

"I try and take each day as it comes and not push myself. I am not looking to get back in to football at the moment. I got really down thinking that I couldn't play anymore. The best thing is to have a clean break from football, but maybe I'll return in the future."

*

"I've left on professional terms. I just think I needed to extend my career on the coaching side."

*

How he was affected by the media obsession with him after the 1990 World Cup:

"I enjoyed the fame and the money coming in, but I didn't like people following around my parents and all the lies that were told about me. In England, they build you up to knock you down. They do that to everyone famous. I was worried about how the public would respond, but luckily they've always been great with me. I don't know why the press have got on my back because I haven't harmed anyone else. If I've done any harm it's only to myself."

*

"I've had to deal with everything but everyone has helped me, including Sir Alex Ferguson, to get through. George Best was a good friend of mine. We loved each other, we both knew where we were coming from."

*

"My Italian's not bad these days. I can understand more than I can speak, but I can still have the odd conversation." (Learnt from his time at Lazio,an Italian football team.)

*

About the hair extensions he got in Italy while at Lazio:

"They looked stupid and it wasn't long before I got rid of them. They only lasted two weeks because every time I had a shower after training it took me about an hour to get dried. I had to cut them out chunk by chunk."

*

"I put some shit in a mince pie. It was cat shit… well actually, no, let's just say it was shit. I took the top off two pies mixed the shit in with the mince before putting the top back on and putting them in the fridge. My two mates came back from a night out and were starving, so both ate a mince pie. One of my mates Jimmy was sick and the other said it was the best mince pie he'd ever had. I laughed for days after that."

*

"I'm going to do things that make me happy. I have always felt that other people are running my life. I don't want that anymore."

*

"I still have my problems but I try and deal with them a bit better now. I don't let them ride on for a month then realise I've got a stack of them."

*

"During the World Cup in 1990, England were flying to Napoli and I said, 'Can I sit in the cockpit?' And they said yeah. So I said to the captain, 'Can I have the controls?' And he said, 'OK, no problem,' and I said, 'How do you get this plane to go right?' And he showed us this button, so I said, 'Can I have a go?' and gave it a little turn, and he went, 'You can give it a bit more,' and I just went whoosh and this plane must have went about three miles off track. And I shit meself. You should have seen the pilot's face while he put it right."

*

"I was practising autographs and the teacher Mr Hepworth said, 'What are you doing that for?' And I said, 'I am going to be a professional footballer.' He said, 'Only one in a million make it' and I said, 'I am going to be that one.' I got kicked out of the classroom.

"After the World Cup in 1990, the only thing I could think of was Mr Hepworth. I knew what class he was in so I went to the school and knocked on his door. I looked in his little window and he looked at us and went, 'I know.'"

*

"And so as I was driving to Manchester I get a phone call from Irving Scholar (chairman of Tottenham): 'Paul, we'll give you £2,500 a week. Not only that, we'll buy your dad a house, so I said, 'Ma and dad, Spurs are gonna buy us a house, what do you think?' 'Sounds good, son.' So I said, 'All right then, yes.'

"Going a bit further, dad calls up, he says, 'Son, what about a car?' and I say, 'Irving, listen, what about a car for me dad, BMW private reg?' 'Yeah, we'll give him that as well.' And now I'm like, 'Dad they're giving us that as well.' I can hear my sister in the background: 'I want a sunbed,' so they threw that in as well."

*

(In 2004 he decided to be known as: 'G8', instead of 'Paul' or 'Gazza' which was a combination of his initial and his football shirt number. The name, however, did not stick.)

"It sounds a bit like great, or it does with my Geordie accent."

*

"From 36 to 42, I wasn't laughing that much. I laugh now just as much as I did when I played football. Yeah."

ON FOOTBALL

"I thought I did well for someone who has been out for 10 or 11 months. Then I was sub against Liverpool and tried to play for the guys and work on my fitness."

*

"At the end of it, I'll maybe do a coaching badge but I'm not going to get forced into things."

*

"I won player of the year and players' player, two cups and two championship medals, had a great time."

*

"But then I always wanted to play for Rangers. Man United is a great club and Alex Ferguson is a legend."

*

"Then all the foreigners started coming over. I don't mind that but a lot of teams are laying out fortunes for ordinary players and that's no good for our youngsters coming through."

*

"I've learnt and I just want to be respected for what I've achieved on the pitch. I know I haven't achieved much off it but I do know I've given pleasure to people watching me play football over the years."

*

"I was thinking Man U is a massive club, so I thought I'll go to Man U – they offered us big wages. Alex Ferguson says, "I'm going on holiday, I'll see you when I get back." "OK, enjoy your holiday, I'll sign." - He didn't.

*

"I don't regret not playing for Manchester United, but at the same time I have thought about that decision a lot. ... I drove to Old Trafford to put pen to paper, but I kept on driving in my car and eventually joined Tottenham."

*

"I enjoyed my time at Spurs, but I do look back and wonder what my life might have been like if I'd signed for United. I reckon Sir Alex Ferguson would have taken me by the balls."

*

"When I was playing for Rangers. The referee was jogging backwards and I said to a couple of my team-mates, "Watch this lads." I bent down and left my leg out as if I was tying my laces and the referee fell over my leg. I winked at the players and we all had a good laugh."

*

"The World Cup was a special time. When I was a young kid playing at my youth club, every night I used to dream about playing football at the World Cup. I lived that dream in Italy, but when I was shown the yellow card I knew it had come to an end. When things are good and I can see they're about to end I get scared, really scared. I couldn't help but cry that night."

*

"I've had 14 bookings this season - 8 of which were my fault, but 7 of which were disputable." (Perhaps Maths isn't his best subject)

*

His feelings about scoring his Wembley goals : the 30-yard free-kick against Arsenal in 1991 & his flick and volley against the Scots at Euro 96

"They both mean something special to me. Firstly, because I am good friends with both the goalkeepers I scored past, David Seaman and Andy Goram, and secondly, because they were both in derbies. The one I scored against Arsenal was brilliant because I'd been out for a while. I told Terry Venables I wouldn't let him down and it made the Spurs fans very happy. Then the one against Scotland was amazing. It was at Wembley for my country and I loved it. Forced to choose, I'd probably go for the one at Euro 96."

*

"The pitch was the only place where I felt safe, secure and good about myself."

*

Gascoigne feels he would have been better staying at

White Hart Lane: "I think I left a bit too early because I was loving it at Spurs. I had everything."

*

"I was proud playing for England in the World Cup. Every game I played in, I did really, really well. I had the world at my feet, you know."

*

"I feel sorry for the fans because they are laying out a lot of money now and if the players don't perform, they are getting robbed of their money."

*

"When I was playing, I wasn't drinking at the weekends. Not after the game, not on Sundays, when I would just relax, have a sauna, things like that."

*

"The chairman is happy, and I am happy. I am 110 percent sure I will sign for Boston United."

*

About when he lunged at Gary Charles in the1991 FA Cup final between Tottenham Hotspur and Nottingham Forest:

"His touch brought him inside and I was off balance. I tried to get a good challenge on him to let him know he was in a game.

"I got up and knew I wasn't feeling right, I got back in the wall and Pearce scored but I wasn't bothered about that. All I was thinking about was my injury.

"The minute I started crying was the minute they started walking up the steps. That was my dream. I still get a lump in my throat when I talk about it. I wasn't bothered with lifting the trophy, I just wanted to walk up those steps.

"A week before that Cup final, I did a coaching video for kids, showing them how to tackle properly otherwise they would do their knee in. But that's exactly what I did. I didn't tackle properly and did my knee in."

*

"After the World Cup in 1990, I knew the pressure would be on me to perform just about in every game because I'd had a good tournament."

*

"If ever I got man of the match, the next game I would tell myself that I had to get man of the match and score. If I scored a couple, the next game I had to get three. That was the way I was. But I was enjoying my football."

*

"People just think of the drinking, that it finished me in football. I was still playing in the premiership, getting man of the match awards every other game, when I was at Everton at 35. Yeah."

*

About the amazing 30-yard free-kick from Gascoigne when Spurs won the FA Cup:

"I remember the free-kick. I didn't know what to do with it. But then Gary Mabbutt came up and said have a shot.

"I used to practise those kicks when I was little. I've caught it absolutely perfectly and it flew in the top corner.

"I could not believe I had caught it so well. I heard the roar and I was off. It doesn't matter what is in front of you, you just want to keep on running.

"Unfortunately, a couple of the lads caught up with me and nailed me to the ground, jumping on me. But I just remember the smile on the face of Terry Venables and the excitement."

*

"I've been told when a player's playing well praise him, and when he's having a bad game fuckin' slaughter him, and I couldn't do that. I couldn't bring myself to slaughter someone having a bad game because I know he's got to sit with his girlfriend or his wife, he knows he's had a bad game, his kid probably thinks, 'Oh, my dad's shit.' Couldn't do it."

*

About football now he's retired:

"I love it. It's frustrating because I need my hip doing. I had titanium put in my hip after the crash and it's moved out of place, so I need that reset. Then I can start running properly. It really hurts at the moment."

*

"I'd like to demonstrate to young kids how to do a move. But until I get my hip fixed, it's limited to what I can show the kids."

ABOUT ALCOHOL AND DRUGS

"But if I wasn't playing, I would drink Saturdays, then Sunday, then Monday. Then I would try and train and it was no good, then have another drink just to pass the day away."

*

"I'll tell you the truth: I had a double brandy before the game but, before, it used to be four bottles of whisky. Not anymore. I was fine. I had a glass of wine after the game. But it was just a mouthful."

*

"The drink? Yes, I've had tough times in my life, especially the last year, regarding my ex-wife, my kids, I nearly broke my neck, I was on death row with pneumonia."

*

"I fought back, got injured again and I had to have another operation. I got down and depressed and I think I was drinking more than I should. Well, I know I was."

*

"You learn, right, a lot of people's problems - why they get upset, why they get down, why they turn to drink - is because they can't say one word and it's N-O, no."

*

"I had to accept that I was an alcoholic, that was the main thing. I think you've got to. But I try not say that I'm an alcoholic. I prefer to say that it's a disease I've got."

*

"I hope I don't die from alcohol because I'll get no sympathy"

*

"Drink or not it's up to me, I could have been in a cemetery. It's been good, bad, even hell, not forgetting another claustrophobic cell.**"**

*

"I went two years without a drink and then....I remember one day in the hospital someone saying I wouldn't make it. I didn't want to die. People say, "Why do you drink?" I don't know, I didn't ask to be an alcoholic in the same way people don't ask to be diabetic."

*

"I'm an alcoholic. I wish I wasn't but I am. I have my bad days and if I have a good day I make the most of it."

*

"I just think sometimes, just think f****** hell. Just go away i.e. drink or me go away – and that means a wooden box and six nails … and I don't know why, I just don't know why I f****** pick up the drink."

*

"Sometimes I think, when am I ever going to learn my lesson?"

*

"I sometimes think I'll be all right with one drink, but then I get too excited and when I'm drunk I'm a nightmare."

*

"I'll tell you the truth: I had a double brandy before the game but, before, it used to be four bottles of whisky. Not any more. I was fine. I had a glass of wine after the game. But it was just a mouthful."

*

"It was there on a plate and I thought I'd try it and I couldn't stop. I locked myself in a hotel room for six weeks. I'd probably have about 16 lines of coke in a day. I went loopy."

*

"I once spent a whole night convinced that a packet of wine gums in my room was staring at me. I was at my Dad's and I woke him up. He told me to eat them. I was so scared it might not work but I did, and from that point onwards the staring stopped.

"Another time I took some money out of a hole in a wall and then ran after a man I was sure had just robbed me. It turned out to be a lamppost. I tackled it so hard I injured myself and went to hospital with internal bleeding. (Speaking about the paranoia drugs can cause)

*

"I was back on the drink for a two-month spell: 'Ah, look at him, he's battling drink, he's going to die.' I've seen people on the drink for years and years, and they're still drinking. I have two months and I'm hammered in the papers."

ON REHAB, STAYING SOBER AND RELAPSING

He describes what happened in rehab in Arizona, in 2013:

"I was dead. I knew I was in a bad way, but I didn't realise it was that bad.

The medics who have spent their careers treating alcoholics said my detox was the worst they had ever seen. I had been pumped with more drugs than any other patient."

*

"I did not think I was going to make it. I've come through that - death."

*

He was moved by the fact that so many helped pay for the rehab he could not now afford :

"Gary Lineker, and a few who didn't wanna be mentioned but they are gonna get mentioned – Wayne Rooney, Steven Gerrard, Jack Wilshere, so I'm going to thank them."

*

He expressed gratitude to his friends, who helped to foot the bill for life-saving treatment in Arizona & spoke about the experience of getting into treatment:

"There was Alan Sugar – usually so tight he cries from one eye – there were a load of people, and Chris Evans was fantastic too he got the ball rolling.

Anything left will be handed back to others who need help.

I had a glass of wine in town and I thought I'm in trouble here I'd better go home.

I woke up with two litres of gin, six bottles of wine and about eight cans, and I thought: 'Oh no, I'm in the s***.

I just thought I'd better get out of here and get to America and detox. But that was it, I was in it and couldn't get myself out.

I blacked out, and I woke up in the treatment centre 16 days later. I was handcuffed to the bed."

*

"You get a lot of people saying, 'I can't go to the match any more because people drink beer there.' Well, fuckin' hell, if that's the case, you may as well just sit in the house for the rest of your life."

*

"I don't know whether I will drink again in my life but I didn't drink yesterday, I am not drinking today and I'll try not to drink again tomorrow."

*

"Now I begin each day with the same statement, "You won't be having a drink today". I'm not ambitious with my goals, but I can admit I'm an alcoholic. That's a start. A year ago I couldn't even say that." (March 2012)

*

"The 11 days spent in the mental hospital were a wake-up call. I observed the others in there and realised I didn't want to end up like them. I heard how George Best died and recognised one of the big consequences if I carried on like I was. I had tried so many times before to stop but I couldn't because I refused to recognise that I was ill.'

*

"I've learned how to do my washing again and my pots in the dishwasher.

..."Now I can do things without a drink. I can play golf, play snooker, go to football, and I don't need a drink inside me first anymore. I go to bars and everyone still offers to buy me a beer.

"The threat is always there. That's why I never say I won't drink again, but I won't drink today." (March 2012, when he had been dry for a year and a half).

*

"When it comes to drinking, I don't look to the future now. Because it only brings worry. I live day by day, a day at a time, as they say."

*

I just know I'm not going to be drinking in the next 10 minutes. I know that for a fact. I don't know about tonight. Any time I get too confident about not drinking, I end up drinking. So I have to stay on my toes."

*

"I've been off pills for three years. I'd be on one lot and when I went to see the psychiatrist, he'd say, 'Who gave you these pills?' and then this other psychiatrist says take these pills, and another says take these. To get rid of you, they just chuck tablets at you. Some treatment centres like to give you titles, like I've got bipolar and all that. Fuckin' 'ell, at one stage I had more titles than Muhammad Ali: you're bipolar, you're OCD, whereas really all I am is an alcoholic. So I don't need any tablets. I feel good."

*

About the 12 step programme in rehab: "I only went to keep people happy. To keep the press happy, to keep my family happy, sometimes to keep my ex-wife happy."

*

"I've done three years before, I've done one year before. The last four years I've been nine months sober every year."

ABOUT BEING A MANAGER

"I do want to be a manager one day. It might be 10 years, I don't know when."

*

"I am going to continue and bring this club forward. I am Paul Gascoigne the footballer."

*

"I like to help create team spirit in the dressing room. I feel that I've got loads of love to give."

*

"Anyway, how can you sack anyone who still hasn't got a contract? I'll be there for the game and I'll stand behind the dugout giving instructions to the players from there. They will respond to me more than the next manager."

WHAT HE HAS SAID ABOUT OTHERS

"I love Jack Charlton. I wish I could be like him.
Every day he wakes up and enjoys his life, but
unfortunately I can't do the same. I find it hard to come to
terms with a lot of things."

*

"Kevin (Wilson) has done a tremendous job here
(Kettering Town) and now it's a matter of trying to work
together and move the team forward. We want to give the
supporters something to look forward to and get them in
the Football League."

*

"I had a great relationship with Chris Waddle, a
Newcastle player who'd already moved to Tottenham and

he told me to come and join him because adored it down there. Then Terry Venables called me up and that impressed me. He promised he would get me in the England squad in three months, but it only took two."

*

Shortly before England's World Cup qualifier with Norway in October 1992, when Gascoigne was asked by Thor Eggen, a reporter, if he wanted to send a message to Norway, he said:

"Yes, fuck off Norway!" (Thor Eggen responded by laughing).

*

How he felt when Glenn Hoddle said he wasn't going to France 98.

"Before I was called in to see Glenn Hoddle, I went into the coaches' room and I saw my pal Glenn Roeder, who had a tear in his eye. At that moment I knew I wasn't going to the World Cup, so I stormed in to Glenn's room and kicked the door down. Phil Neville came running out and I just started calling Glenn all the names under the sun.

"I started throwing things at him and smashing things up. Glenn was saying, "Let me explain", but there was nothing to explain. I helped him get to the World Cup in the qualifiers, especially with that 0-0 in Italy. If I hadn't played in that game, maybe I wouldn't have been so angry.

And then Glenn did a double-page spread in a newspaper. "When I see him these days I try to shake his hand, although he wasn't happy when I described what had happened between us in my book. He was very upset about it and he wouldn't shake my hand. Hopefully he's over that now."

*

When Gascoigne was asked, in 2005, if he had a message for Norway he answered:

"Yeah, and it's not 'fuck off' this time. I want Norwegians to know that they have a beautiful, clean country, although I'm glad I'm not still drinking because it's about £8 for a half a lager over there! It's so expensive. When I told them to 'fuck off' I didn't really mean it. I was just fed up of the press asking me stupid questions."

*

"Wayne Rooney is a fantastic player who wants to win every game. It is his determination which is coming to the fore. Unfortunately, things like that happened to me many years ago when I had a go at the referee. I did daft things and I once got booked for showing a ref the red card. But the rules have changed now, and if you applaud the ref that is what happens."

*

The best managers he feels he has played under

"Terry Venables and Walter Smith. Terry was a genius, he was a manager and a coach. He was great with me. Walter was tough, but he gave me my space. I loved both of them and really appreciated what they did for me."

*

When in a New Zealand hotel, Gascoigne was told there was no bacon for breakfast, he exclaimed:

"What, all the sheep in this country and there's no bloody bacon!"

*

"I think Harry (Redknapp) would be a brilliant England manager because he has the respect of the players and that's all you need in that job."

*

"Coisty's (Ally McCoist) blue through and through. I hope either new backers give him £30million or, better still, he goes down the same route Sir Alex Ferguson did with Beckham, Giggs, the Nevilles and Scholes and gets half-a-dozen young Scottish kids to become the new core of the team."

*

"Wayne Rooney needs to get nasty again, He's toned down too much and he's not quite the player he was. I'm not saying he should be breaking people's legs but the aggressive Rooney is the best Rooney."

*

'Stevie Gerrard, I can guarantee you, will have sought out Kenny Dalglish after his hat-trick ...against Everton and still asked his boss if he played OK. That's what I used to do and I recognise the same kind of person and player in him."

*

..."I might get hold of Scott Parker and tell him he's a great player but instead of always releasing the ball at the first opportunity to try something different and give it a go."

*

"The Rangers player Gordon Durie had stitched me up over something, so I asked to borrow his car after training one day. I'd been fishing early that morning, and I had a couple of trout with me. I put one in the boot. I knew that's where he would look once the smell started. But I squeezed the second one in between the back seat and the floor. A couple of days later, Durie handed me the trout from the boot. 'Good try, mate.'

"Three or four days after, he came up to us again: 'My car still stinks. I can't understand it.' When he found out, he went mental, but it was worth it. The chairman wasn't too chuffed, though. The car was a sponsored one, provided by the club. I think it had to be scrapped."

ABOUT HIS OCD AND FEAR OF FLYING

"I'm OK now. It was mostly nerves. I used to be very nervous when I woke up on the morning of a game. It was only when I got my football boots on in the dressing room that I felt fine because that was my home. OCD's a very tough thing to conquer and I think I have it under control now. I have a few lapses, but I'm OK. It's all in the mind."

*

I had to touch it. You cannot explain the feeling, it's just something that you have. Tapping the doors is just something I had to do, But hopefully that's some good luck for them. The medication slows down the symptoms. I could come off the medication now if I want to, but if it's going to stop me from, like, touching things nine times and mean I only touch them three times... Thank God it was not 27 times. It used to be five, then it was seven, then it was nine.

*

He talked about his fear of flying, on a plane to join the Football Association HIV awareness effort in Botswana in 2006, a fear which began when he experienced turbulence during a flight from New Zealand to Fiji, in1986:

The plane dropped 800ft in a couple of seconds and the food hit the ceiling. People say the time to worry is when the air stewardesses start crying, and every one of them was crying, so I got really scared. It's only weeks since the police raids that allegedly foiled a plot to blow up transatlantic planes, and this isn't helping. I'm more scared this time than I probably have been before.

*

"Sometimes I've locked the door of the house, got 20 miles up the motorway, turned round, come back and checked the door again."

*

"I got cured 90% now. I was touching the door handles nine times, shoes off and on, numbers, and when I was in the Priory they got this guy in and he made us do all the things I'd do the opposite way. I had 30-odd hours with him and now when I shut the door I just shut it the normal way. It was horrible, but I got through it… I used to do all the cracks in the pavement, and I've stopped all that."

*

'I always put my left shoe on and then my right but they made me do it the other way round.'

*

I was working out on the floor of the hospital. I was doing 1,600 squats, 800 press-ups and 900 sit-ups every day."

DAVE FARNHAM

WHAT OTHERS HAVE SAID ABOUT HIM

George Best:

"I once said Gazza's IQ was less than his shirt number and he asked me: "What's an IQ?""

*

Former girlfriend, Jenny, nicknamed 'Fruit' by Gazza:

"All the signs were there. Paul was drinking 24 hours a day, was taking a gram of cocaine almost every night and began to act very weird - crazy even.

I'm so glad he's now getting the help he needs. It's so sad that he has been sectioned but I saw it coming. He has been hitting the self-destruct button for a long time. The more time I spent with Paul, the more I noticed a change in him. He became wired and unpredictable and would flip and turn violent over nothing. He was uncontrollable.

If it wasn't for his family, who he loves very much, I think Paul would be dead by now. He even cried before and after sex.

He was so much fun. We'd go out to bars and he'd order three or four bottles of Dom Perignon and we'd get blind drunk. He loved music and we'd go to music bars where he'd ask me to get him cocaine and we smoked spliffs together.

He kept pestering me to be his full-time girlfriend but I refused because I was with someone else. Yes, we were more than friends and we did have sex but I didn't ever class myself as his girlfriend.

He'd pay me £100 just to sit with him in the casino. I'd get bored but he'd get angry if I said I wanted to leave.

...At night, he liked to drink wine or champagne. I saw him drink for 18 hours solid until he collapsed. He went heavy on the drugs too.

He would get the biggest cigars you can buy and dip them in his brandy. He'd only ever smoke a bit and then give it a stranger.

He didn't eat. I've never seen Paul finish a full meal. He only ever ate a little bit and was bulimic. I made him dinner at my house once and he made himself throw up in the bathroom. There was blood everywhere.

...He came over to mine and we drank and smoked pot and ended up sleeping together.

Paul had these weird superstitions, even in sex. We were in bed and I started grabbing him with my hands and he shouted, 'STOP!' He told me I was only ever to use my left hand to touch him.

I was shocked. It was totally bizarre. He insisted both of us only used our left hands. I thought he was just joking but he was serious.

He then blurted out some nonsense that we would be cursed and aliens will come and get us if we didn't use just our left hands. It was plain weird

...I was with a female friend and we were all smoking pot.

Paul rang his pal Jimmy 'Five Bellies' and bragged that he was going to have a threesome. He kept asking me and my friend to kiss each other.

Then he came into the lounge completely naked and started having sex with my mop. We laughed but it was a bit disturbing. He then asked if we could all have sex together and we said no.

He went crazy. He had this big watch on and threw it against the wall. He was screaming and shouting and left, taking the door off its hinges as he slammed it.

He threatened to kill me if I ever went to the papers. I remember him saying, 'My dad's the hardest man in the Toon'. I didn't doubt it and I was scared.

I don't think Paul would ever have hurt me. It was the drink talking.

...He lost so much weight, his muscles were wasting away. He looked ill.

...They (his fans) loved him. I never heard anyone say anything bad to him and he always signed autographs.

I always blamed it on the alcohol. But in the end, I had enough of being around him.

He became a sad recluse just drinking himself stupid in his room for days on end.

He's the kind of person you want to take to the middle of Scotland and tie him to a tree until he gets better.

I hope that now with some professional help he can heal but, unfortunately, the only person who can help Paul is himself."

*

Newcastle United defender, John Bailey said of Gascoigne, who was a young team member at the time, that he was:

"either going to be one of the greats or finish up at 40, bitter about wasting such talent".

*

Glenn Roeder captained the Magpies (Newcastle United) on their last tour of the Oceanian island country back in 1985. He was in a side which had Paul Gascoigne in it as well. Gascoigne was a goalscorer for the Magpies. He refers to an incident that occurred in New Zealand:

"We lost Gazza in Napier for a while. He disappeared and then he turned up but we couldn't recognise him. He's only gone and got his hair bleached blond! But that was Gazza. He just used to get bored and go and do daft things like that."

*

Stan Seymour, chairman of Newcastle United, after Gascoigne had been in trouble with the law, said he was like:

"George Best without brains."

*

Gary Lineker tweeted:

"Lots of you asking for my thoughts on Gazza's plight. I can only hope he finds peace somehow, but fear those hopes may be forlorn."

*

His agent Terry Baker said:

"His life is always in danger because he is an alcoholic. Maybe no one can save him - I don't know. I really don't know."

*

Ronnie Irani, cricketer, who was among the celebrities who helped fund his rehab in 2013:

"He is getting his life on track, but it really is down to him now.

The treatment has given him a second chance – he has to take it."

*

Gary Lineker, also helped to finance the rehab in 2013 and he remembers when they they made an advert, in 1996, for Walkers Crisps:

"They had this contraption under his eyes and it was spurting out the tears. It was so funny.

The pair of us could not stop laughing. In his prime, Gazza was bright and witty, and I think that has been dulled by what he has been going through.

Along with others, I am trying to do something to help – but ultimately, it is going to have to come from him.

This time Paul has reached that so-called rock bottom and hopefully it will force him to try. But there needs to be a reason to want to get better.

I have always worried that for Gazza, without his football, what would that reason be?"

*

Neil Cameron, journalist:

"Gascoigne is anything but selfish. In fact, if he had thought more about himself, rather than being a people pleaser, then he might have ended up a bit happier. There are many reasons why his life has spiralled out of control. One of them is because he allowed people to take advantage of him, as they made everything about his generous nature."

*

Paul Ince, footballer:

"The best player I've ever played with was Paul Gascoigne. He had everything. He was amazing."

*

Terry Venables, Manager of Spurs, on hearing about Gascoigne signing a contract with Lazio said:

"I'm very pleased for Paul but it's like watching your mother-in-law drive off a cliff in your new car."

*

Glen Hoddle, manager:

"My saddest decision in football was leaving Paul Gascoigne out of the 1998 World Cup finals.

But he wasn't fit enough and once that decision is made, as a manager and a group of players, you forget about who isn't there and focus on the job."

*

The Daily Mirror showed a photo of Paul Gascoigne on their front page, on 22 August 2014; the headline read:

"Help me, I'm in trouble"

.

Paul Gascoigne was shown getting into an ambulance after being found slumped over with a bottle of gin

*

Ally McCoist, Glasgow Rangers manager:

"Paul just looks a poor soul and everyone has real major

concerns as to where this is going to go. It is not good."

*

Paul Gascoigne's sister, Lindsay, wrote on Facebook:

"This illness is so tragic and there is no cure and has shown its ugly head again.

Please leave us alone to grieve and pull together as a family as always to help save a great man."

*

Michael Barrymore, TV presenter, tweeted:

"If anyone out there knows how I can contact Paul Gascoigne, please let me know.

It is never, never, never too late."

*

Oueen's Park Rangers' manager, Harry Redknapp:

"He is a great lad and it is just sad to see how he is looking at the moment. I saw him about a month ago and I said: 'I will pick you up in the mornings Gazza, come training with me. Do a little bit of work with the kids.

I would love it if he would do that, if he wants to do it I

would pick him up every morning at 5.45am at the end of his road and bring him in. He could go and do some coaching with the kids. That is an open invitation to him.

I see Gazza around and he is such a lovely boy, he has got a heart of gold.

He has probably given his last penny away but that is just how he is.

Everyone has tried to help him but the only person who can help him now is himself."

*

John Gibson. Chronicle Live:

"A Geordie with an impish sense of humour and a heart of pure gold, he was a clown with a tear never far from the corner of his eye.

"The greatest English footballing genius of his generation, Gazza was equally tormented by injuries and demons. It was said that Stella Artois became his girlfriend as he self destructed in an orgy of booze, drugs, pain and the mind-gripping obsessive compulsive disorder.

"Maybe but one thing always shone through the confusion. Gazza was a ruddy brilliant footballer. And he was totally, wonderfully ours. All ours.

"I've known Paul throughout his long and colourful journey, from a fresh faced cheeky kid receiving a trophy from me at the local social club, through his great years when I visited him at his luxury villa in Rome, on to late in his playing days when he magnificently came riding to my rescue in helping raise funds to save Gateshead, his home town football club. Through dentist chairs, broken hearts, and futile redemption.

"I have a treasure chest full of happy memories and they are the ones I prefer to concentrate on at the expense of the more lurid. That he now stands on the brink of a dark abyss is little short of a tragedy."

*

Bobby Robson, former England manager, said about Paul Gascoigne that he was:

"Daft as a brush"

*

Mirandinha, a Newcastle player referred to Gascoigne as:

"The crazy one."

*

Steve Spiegel, who runs a rehab centre:

"He was emaciated. He was completely lost. I think he felt hopeless and helpless; just a little boy running about. He didn't know where to turn and who to trust. He'd been ripped off so many times, and part of that was down to him. Let's be fair, what he wants is to be loved. And he's a lovely human being."

*

Ray Clemence England goalkeeper:

"Mastery of the ball was boring for Gazza. Volleying the ball into the net from 30 yards out? He'd do it. In the end, he'd say, 'I know I'll do it with my eyes closed.' He'd do that too. He'd try to find different ways to miskick the ball into the net."

*

Birmingham manager Lee Clark:

"If Paul Gascoigne had not done his knee, he would have become the best player in the world."

*

Franz Beckenbauer, German footballer:

"A true footballer of the streets – defiant, crafty and intrepid. He could cook up ideas you didn't expect."

OTHER BOOKS BY DAVE FARNHAM

Snippets of Boris Johnson

Snippets of Nigel Farage

Snippets of Jeremy Kyle

Snippets of Joan Rivers

Snippets of Richard Attenborough

Snippets of Billy Connolly